Love FRIES

A collection of high-fryers!

First published in 2013
LOVE FOOD is an imprint of Parragon Books Ltd

Parragon
Chartist House
15–17 Trim Street
Bath, BA1 1HA, UK

ISBN: 978-1-4723-0207-6

Printed in China

Photography by Mike Cooper
Home economy by Lincoln Jefferson
New recipes and introduction by Robin Donovan
Edited by Fiona Biggs

Notes for the Reader
This book uses standard kitchen measuring spoons and cups. All spoon and cup measurements are level unless otherwise indicated. Unless otherwise stated, milk is assumed to be whole, butter is assumed to be salted, eggs are large, individual vegetables are medium, and pepper is freshly ground black pepper. Unless otherwise stated, all root vegetables should be washed and peeled before using. For the best results, use a meat thermometer when cooking meat and poultry—check the latest USDA government guidelines for current advice.

Garnishes and serving suggestions are all optional and not necessarily included in the recipe ingredients or method. The times given are only an approximate guide. Preparation times differ according to the techniques used by different people and the cooking times may also vary from those given. Optional ingredients, variations, or serving suggestions have not been included in the calculations. Some of the recipes in this book call for some additional kitchen equipment that can be purchased in kitchen-supply stores.

Recipes using raw or very lightly cooked eggs should be avoided by infants, the elderly, pregnant women, and people with weakened immune systems. Pregnant and breast-feeding women are advised to avoid eating peanuts and peanut products. People with nut allergies should be aware that some of the prepared ingredients used in the recipes in this book may contain nuts. Always check the packaging before use.

Contents

"DO YOU WANT THAT WITH FRIES?"

Once a question asked only at fast-food restaurant counters, these days you're just as likely to hear it while sitting at a table set with white linen and fine china. The humble fry, it seems, is returning to its roots in the birthplace of haute cuisine.

THE HISTORY

Both the French and their Belgian neighbors claim responsibility for creating the delectable french fry. What's important, however, is that at some fated moment in the early part of the nineteenth century, an anonymous and unsung culinary genius, somewhere in Europe, had the bright idea of slicing a potato into sticks and dropping them into a saucepan of hot oil to produce a delectable snack.

By the 1830s, the irresistible deep-fried potatoes had become a popular item in both France and Belgium. By World War I, street vendors throughout Europe were selling them from specially equipped trucks and American soldiers stationed in those parts quickly succumbed to their addictive powers. When those soldiers returned to the United States, their hunger gave birth to the fast-food industry. The rest, as they say, is history.

Since then, these perfect potato creations have spread around the world and have earned the cultlike devotion of children and adults alike. The current restaurant love affair with all things kitsch has also fueled a revival of sorts. These days, you'll find them adorned with everything from simple salt to spicy chili to prohibitively pricey French truffles.

ESSENTIAL INGREDIENTS

Years of history have produced a veritable mountain of knowledge about the best ingredients to use. There are, of course, only two essential ingredients, potatoes and oil, but it is key to get these two correct.

POTATOES—It all starts with a great frying potato, one that is high in starch and low in moisture: in other words, the russet. Peeling or not is purely a question of personal preference.

OIL—A full-flavored cooking fat with a high smoke point is also a must. Lard and rendered duck fat are ideal for deep-frying, but less expensive oils, such as peanut, canola, corn, or simply "vegetable" oils are fine substitutes. For the best of both worlds, combine a rich animal fat with an inexpensive vegetable oil.

COOKING METHODS

Our favorite cooking method, which is described in the Hand-Cut Fries recipe (page 10), is for the potatoes to be double-fried in a combination of beef suet and vegetable oil, but you can use vegetable shortening to replace the suet. We have given two methods for cooking our Hand-Cut Fries:

DEEP-FRYING—An electric deep-fryer minimizes the work and mess associated with deep-frying, but a heavy saucepan on the stove fitted with an inexpensive deep-frying thermometer will work just as well.

OVEN-BAKING—This is a great way to make healthier but equally delicious fries. If you don't have a deep-fryer or don't want to cook with hot oil, this is a simple way to cook light and crisp fries easily.

Once you master the basic method, there's no limit to the imaginative toppings, seasonings, and dips that you can add to dress up your fries. Perhaps the pertinent question today isn't "Would you like that with fries?" but instead, "Would you like your fries with that or that or that?"

TIPS FOR PREPARATION

—Some of the recipes in this book call for some additional kitchen equipment, which can be purchased in kitchen supply stores or from online sources.

—Soak the cut potatoes in water before cooking to prevent them from clumping and to make sure they form a desirable crisp shell and creamy interior.

—Wrap the cut potatoes in a clean dish towel to draw out any excess water.

TIPS FOR DEEP-FRYING

—Never leave hot oil unattended. If you are using a saucepan of oil, don't overfill it; there should be at least 2 inches from the top of the oil to the rim of the pan.

—When adding the sliced potatoes, be careful not to overcrowd the saucepan, because this will reduce the temperature of the oil.

—Make sure the oil is kept at the correct temperature because this will ensure perfect crispness.

—After cooking, let the fries drain on paper towels to absorb any excess oil.

TIPS FOR OVEN-BAKING

—To make sure all the sliced potatoes are lightly coated with oil, without using too much, put them in a clean plastic food bag. Add 2 tablespoons of vegetable oil and 1 teaspoon of salt, then, making sure the bag is sealed, give the bag and its contents a light shake to coat the potatoes.

—Use a large, preheated baking sheet and spread the cut potatoes out in a single layer to make sure they cook evenly.

Hand-Cut Fries

SERVES **4**   PREP **15**   COOK **10** MINUTES

INGREDIENTS

8 russet potatoes
(about 2 pounds)

2 cups vegetable oil

2 cups beef suet or
vegetable shortening

sea salt, to taste

1. Peel the potatoes, if desired, and cut into ¼ x ¼-inch sticks. Soak in a bowl of cold water for 5 minutes, then drain, rinse, and wrap in a clean dish towel to dry.

2. Place the oil and suet in a large, heavy saucepan or a deep-fryer. If using a saucepan, attach a deep-frying thermometer. Heat the oil mixture to 350–375°F, or until a cube of bread browns in 30 seconds. Carefully add the cut potatoes, in batches, if necessary, to avoid overcrowding. Cook for about 3–4 minutes, until beginning to brown. Remove using tongs and drain on a plate lined with paper towels.

3. Reheat the oil to 350–375°F, then add the potatoes and fry for 3–5 minutes, until golden brown and crisp. Remove from the oil and drain on a plate lined with paper towels. Season generously with sea salt and serve immediately.

Variation: If you're interested in lightening up your fries, baking in an oven is a great alternative. Preheat the oven to 450°F. Toss the cut potatoes with 2 tablespoons of vegetable oil and 1 teaspoon of salt. Spread the fries in a single layer on a large baking sheet and bake in the preheated oven for about 30 minutes, turning them over halfway through cooking, until they are golden brown and crisp.

Beef suet adds flavor to this classic homemade
french fry recipe. If you don't want to use suet,
or vegetable shortening, use all vegetable oil
(Just double the quantity).

Shoestring Fries

SERVES   PREP   COOK

4   10   4 MINUTES

INGREDIENTS

8 russet potatoes
(about 2 pounds)

4 cups vegetable oil

sea salt, to taste

1. Slice the potatoes into thin strips using a handheld julienne peeler or the julienne attachment on a handheld mandoline. Put the sliced potatoes into a bowl of cold water and let soak for 5 minutes. Drain, rinse, and wrap tightly in a clean dish towel, squeezing over the sink to remove as much water as possible.

2. Place the oil in a large, heavy saucepan or a deep-fryer. If using a saucepan, attach a deep-frying thermometer. Heat the oil to 350–375°F, or until a cube of bread browns in 30 seconds. Carefully add the cut potatoes, in batches, if necessary, to avoid overcrowding. Cook for 3–4 minutes, until golden brown and crisp. Remove using tongs and drain on a plate lined with paper towels. Season generously with sea salt and serve immediately.

Thin shreds of potato are quickly fried into a crunchy and addictive tangle that looks great on a plate or piled on top of a sandwich.

Sweet Potato Fries

SERVES **4** PREP **10** COOK **4** MINUTES

INGREDIENTS

4 cups vegetable oil

½ cup all-purpose flour, plus extra if needed

1 teaspoon salt

1 cup water, plus extra if needed

6 orange-flesh sweet potatoes (about 2 pounds), peeled and cut into ¼-inch sticks

sea salt, to taste

1. Place the oil in a large, heavy saucepan or a deep-fryer. If using a saucepan, attach a deep-frying thermometer. Heat the oil to 350–375°F, or until a cube of bread browns in 30 seconds.

2. Meanwhile, combine the flour and salt in a medium bowl. Beat in the water until well combined. The batter should be the consistency of a thin pancake batter. If it is too thick, add more water, 1 tablespoon at a time. If it is too thin, add more flour, 1 tablespoon at a time.

3. Add a handful of the sweet potatoes to the batter and stir to coat. Remove from the batter using tongs, letting the excess drip back into the bowl. Transfer the battered potatoes to the hot oil and cook for 3–4 minutes, until golden brown and crisp. Remove using tongs and drain on a plate lined with paper towels. Continue cooking, in batches, if necessary, until all of the potatoes are cooked. Season generously with salt and serve immediately.

Sweet potatoes are packed with nutrition, making this sinfully delicious treat just a tiny bit more virtuous.

Triple-Cooked Fries

SERVES   PREP   COOK

4   10   15 MINUTES

PLUS CHILLING

INGREDIENTS

8 russet potatoes
(about 2 pounds)

4 cups vegetable oil

sea salt, to taste

1. Cut the potatoes into ¼ x ¼-inch sticks. Soak the cut potatoes in a bowl of cold water for 5 minutes, then drain and rinse.

2. Bring a medium-sized saucepan of lightly salted water to the boil over a high heat. Add the potatoes, bring back to the boil and cook for 3–4 minutes, until the potatoes begin to soften. Drain the potatoes and spread on a baking sheet lined with paper towels. Refrigerate for 1 hour or overnight.

3. Place the oil in a large, heavy saucepan or a deep-fryer. If using a saucepan, attach a deep-frying thermometer. Heat the oil to 350–375°F, or until a cube of bread browns in 30 seconds. Carefully add the cut potatoes, in batches, if necessary, to avoid overcrowding. Cook for about 3–4 minutes, until beginning to brown. Remove using tongs and drain on a plate lined with paper towels.

4. Reheat the oil to 350–375°F, then add the potatoes again and fry for about 3–5 minutes, until golden brown and crisp. Remove from the oil and drain on a plate lined with paper towels. Season generously with sea salt and serve immediately.

For fries that are soft and fluffy inside and light and crispy on the outside, triple cooking—once in water and twice in oil—is the key.

Seasoned Curly Fries

SERVES **4** PREP **10** COOK **4** MINUTES

INGREDIENTS

8 russet potatoes
(about 2 pounds)

vegetable oil, for frying

¼ cup all-purpose flour,
plus extra if needed

¾ teaspoon garlic powder

1 teaspoon salt

1½ teaspoons paprika

½–¾ teaspoon
cayenne pepper

1½ cups beer,
plus extra if needed

sea salt, to taste

1. Using a spiral vegetable cutter, cut the potatoes into spirals. Separate the spirals into individual strands. If you end up with just a few very long spirals, cut them into more manageable pieces.

2. Place the oil in a large, heavy saucepan or a deep-fryer. If using a saucepan, attach a deep-frying thermometer. Heat the oil to 350–375°F, or until a cube of bread browns in 30 seconds.

3. Meanwhile, combine the flour, garlic powder, salt, paprika, and cayenne pepper in a large bowl. Beat in the beer. The batter should be the consistency of a thin pancake batter. If it is too thick, add more beer, 1 tablespoon at a time. If it is too thin, add more flour, 1 tablespoon at a time.

4. Working in small batches, drop the potato spirals into the batter and swish them around to thoroughly coat. Remove using tongs, letting the excess drip back into the bowl. Drop the battered spirals into the hot oil and cook for 3–4 minutes, until brown and crisp. Using tongs, transfer the cooked fries to a plate lined with paper towels, sprinkle with sea salt, and continue cooking, in batches, if necessary, until all of the fries are cooked.

If using a deep-fryer, dunk the basket in the oil before adding the battered fries to prevent them from sticking to it.

Cheesy Fries

SERVES **4** PREP **20** COOK **15** MINUTES

INGREDIENTS

3 tablespoons butter

3 tablespoons all-purpose flour

1½ cups milk

3 cups shredded cheddar cheese,

½ cup sour cream

2 teaspoons Dijon mustard

½ teaspoon salt

freshly cooked Hand-Cut Fries (see page 10)

1. Melt the butter in a saucepan over a medium heat. Whisk in the flour and cook for a further 30 seconds. Slowly add the milk and cook over a medium heat, whisking constantly, for a further 3 minutes, until the sauce thickens. Reduce the heat to low and add the cheese a little at a time, stirring after each addition until the cheese is completely melted. Stir in the sour cream, mustard and salt. Keep the sauce warm until ready to serve.

2. Place the fries in a large bowl or on a serving platter and pour the sauce over them (or, if you prefer, serve the sauce in a bowl on the side for dipping). Serve immediately.

Our classic Hand-Cut Fries topped with a luscious layer of cheese sauce—delicious!

Garlic Fries

SERVES **PREP** **COOK**
4 **20** **10** MINUTES

INGREDIENTS

1 tablespoon olive oil

3 large garlic cloves, finely chopped

2 tablespoons finely chopped fresh flat-leaf parsley

freshly cooked Hand-Cut Fries (see page 10)

sea salt, to taste

1. Beat together the oil, garlic, and parsley in a large bowl.

2. Toss the hot fries with the garlic mixture. Season generously with sea salt and serve immediately.

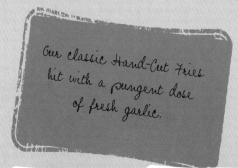

Our classic Hand-Cut Fries hit with a pungent dose of fresh garlic.

Root Vegetable Fries

SERVES **4**   PREP **10**   COOK **25** MINUTES

INGREDIENTS

2 pounds any combination of parsnips, rutabagas, turnips, and carrots, peeled and cut into ¼-inch sticks

2 tablespoons vegetable oil

1 teaspoon salt

sea salt, to taste

1. Preheat the oven to 450°F.

2. Toss the cut vegetables with the oil and salt. Spread the vegetables in a single layer on a large baking sheet and bake in the preheated oven for about 20 minutes, flipping them halfway through cooking, until they are golden brown and cooked through. Remove from the oven and preheat the broiler to medium.

3. Place under the preheated broiler for 2–3 minutes, until they begin to become crisp. Turn them over and return them to the broiler for an additional 2 minutes, until the other side is crisp. Serve immediately, sprinkled with sea salt.

Who says fries need to be made from potatoes? Our delicious Root Vegetable Fries are made from parsnips, rutabagas, turnips, and carrots.

Bacon & Cheese Fries

SERVES **4** PREP **30** COOK **25** MINUTES

INGREDIENTS

3 bacon strips

3 tablespoons butter

½ onion, diced

1 garlic clove, finely chopped

3 tablespoons all-purpose flour

1½ cups milk

2½ cups shredded cheddar cheese, American cheese, or Monterey Jack cheese

⅔ cup freshly grated Parmesan cheese

½ cup sour cream

2 teaspoons Dijon mustard

½ teaspoon salt

freshly cooked Hand-Cut Fries (see page 10)

2 tablespoons snipped fresh chives, to garnish

1. Fry the bacon in a dry skillet until crisp, then remove and drain on paper towels. Crumble and set aside.

2. Melt the butter in a saucepan over medium heat. Add the onion and cook, stirring, for about 4 minutes, until soft. Add the garlic and cook for an additional minute. Beat in the flour and cook for an additional 30 seconds. Slowly add the milk and cook over medium heat, beating continuously, for an additional 3 minutes, until the sauce thickens. Reduce the heat to low and add the cheddar cheese and Parmesan cheese ¼ cup at a time, stirring after each addition, until the cheeses are completely melted. Stir in the sour cream, mustard, and salt. Keep the sauce warm until ready to serve.

3. Place the fries in a large bowl or on a serving platter and pour the sauce over them. Sprinkle with the crumbled bacon and chives and serve immediately.

Just when you thought cheesy fries couldn't get any better, we've pumped up the flavor with onion, garlic, two kinds of cheese, crumbled bacon, and fresh chives.

Nacho Fries

SERVES **4** PREP **10** COOK **15** MINUTES

INGREDIENTS

6 russet potatoes
(about 1½ pounds),
scrubbed or peeled and
cut into thin circles

6 cups vegetable oil

2 cups shredded, cooked,
chicken breast

2 cups shredded cheddar
cheese, American cheese,
or Monterey Jack cheese

½ cup sliced, pickled
jalapeños

½ cup Spicy Salsa
(see page 78)

½ cup sour cream

salt, to taste

1. Soak the sliced potatoes in a large bowl of cold water for about
5 minutes. Drain and rinse, then spread out in a single layer on a clean
dish towel. Top with another clean dish towel and press to absorb the
excess water.

2. Place the oil in a large, heavy saucepan or a deep-fryer. If using a
saucepan, attach a deep-frying thermometer. Heat the oil to 350–375°F,
or until a cube of bread browns in 30 seconds. Carefully add the cut
potatoes, in batches, if necessary, to avoid overcrowding. Cook for about
5–6 minutes, until golden brown and crisp. Remove using tongs and drain
on a plate lined with kitchen paper. Season with salt.

3. Preheat the oven to 450°F and spread the cooked potato slices in a
large baking dish. Top the potatoes with the chicken and cheese and cook
in the preheated oven for about 5 minutes, until the cheese is melted and
bubbling. Remove from the oven and top with the jalapeños, salsa, and
sour cream. Serve immediately.

For a hearty snack full of Mexican flavor, cook up this potato-based version of nachos. Use leftover meat or broil a seasoned, boneless, skinless chicken breast.

Cajun Fries

SERVES **PREP** **COOK**
4 **15** **10** MINUTES

INGREDIENTS

1 tablespoon paprika

2 teaspoons salt

2 teaspoons garlic powder

1 teaspoon freshly ground
black pepper

1 teaspoon cayenne pepper

1 teaspoon lightly crushed
dried oregano

1 teaspoon lightly crushed
thyme

freshly cooked Hand-Cut
Fries (see page 10)

1. Combine the paprika, salt, garlic powder, black pepper, cayenne pepper, oregano, and thyme in a small bowl.

2. Toss the cooked fries with the spice mix and serve immediately.

add a kick to your fries with a fiery Cajun spice mix.

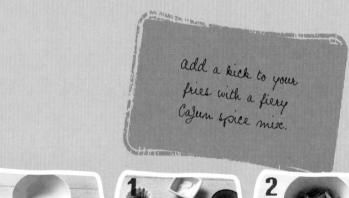

Chili con Carne Fries

SERVES **4**

PREP **30** MINUTES

COOK **1** HOUR **20** MINUTES

INGREDIENTS

2 tablespoons vegetable oil

1 onion, diced

3 garlic cloves, finely chopped

2 pounds fresh ground beef

3 tablespoons tomato paste

3 tablespoons hot or mild chili powder, or to taste

2 tablespoons paprika

1 tablespoon dried cumin

1 tablespoon crumbled dried oregano

1 teaspoon salt

½ teaspoon ground cinnamon

¼ teaspoon ground cloves

1 (28-ounce) can diced tomatoes, with their juices

½ cup beef stock or chicken stock

1½ cups beer

freshly cooked Hand-Cut Fries (see page 10)

2 cups shredded cheddar cheese, to serve (optional)

1. Heat the oil in a skillet over medium–high heat. Add the onion and garlic and cook, stirring frequently, for about 5 minutes, until soft. Add the ground beef and cook, breaking up the meat with a spatula, for about 5 minutes, until brown. Drain the excess fat from the skillet.

2. Stir in the tomato paste, chili powder, paprika, cumin, oregano, salt, cinnamon, and cloves and cook, stirring, for an additional minute. Stir in the tomatoes with their juices, stock, and beer. Bring to a boil, reduce the heat to medium–low, and simmer, stirring occasionally, for about 1 hour, until the mixture is thick and most of the liquid has evaporated. Keep warm until ready to serve (or refrigerate for up to two days and reheat on the stove before serving).

3. Place the fries in individual serving bowls and top each with a hearty serving of chili and a sprinkling of cheese, if using. Serve immediately.

Fries drenched in spicy chili are a cold-weather favorite. This flavorsome chili is even better if you make it a day or two ahead.

Coconut Curry Fries

SERVES **4**   PREP **35**   COOK **40** MINUTES

INGREDIENTS

freshly cooked Hand-Cut
Fries (see page 10)

¼ cup finely chopped
fresh cilantro

FRIED SHALLOTS

6 cups vegetable oil

2 shallots, thinly sliced

1 teaspoon
all-purpose flour

sea salt, to taste

SAUCE

2 tablespoons olive oil

1 shallot, diced

4 teaspoons
Thai red curry paste

2 tablespoons
Thai fish sauce

2 tablespoons packed
light brown sugar

1¾ cups canned
coconut milk

2 tablespoons lime juice

1. To make the fried shallots, place the oil into a large, heavy saucepan or a deep-fryer. If using a saucepan, attach a deep-frying thermometer. Heat the oil to 350–375°F, or until a cube of bread browns in 30 seconds. While the oil is heating, toss the sliced shallots with the flour. Carefully add the shallots to the oil, in batches, if necessary, to avoid overcrowding. Cook for about 1 minute, until golden brown and crisp (watch them carefully because they can quickly burn). Remove, using tongs, drain on a plate lined with paper towels, and generously season with sea salt. (The fried shallots can be stored in the refrigerator in a tightly covered container for up to a week, but bring to room temperature before using.)

2. To make the sauce, heat the oil in a large skillet over medium–high heat. Add the shallot and cook, stirring occasionally, for about 5 minutes, until soft. Add the curry paste, fish sauce, and sugar and cook, stirring, for about 1 minute. Add the coconut milk and bring to a boil. Reduce the heat to low and simmer for 15–20 minutes, until the sauce is thick and the flavors have come together. Stir in the lime juice. Keep warm until ready to serve.

3. Arrange the fries on a serving platter and drizzle the sauce over the top. Garnish with the fried shallots and chopped cilantro and serve immediately.

Crispy fries are topped with a rich, spicy coconut milk curry sauce, fresh cilantro, and crunchy fried shallots.

Pulled Pork Fries

SERVES 4
PREP 25 MINUTES
COOK 6 HOURS 10 MINUTES

INGREDIENTS

1 large onion, thinly sliced

4 teaspoons packed light brown sugar

4 teaspoons paprika

3 pounds bone-in pork shoulder

⅔ cup cider vinegar

¼ cup Worcestershire sauce

1 teaspoon crushed red pepper

1 tablespoon sugar

1 teaspoon dry mustard

2 garlic cloves, finely chopped

freshly cooked Hand-Cut Fries (see page 10)

salt and pepper

COLESLAW

¼ cup cider vinegar

1 tablespoon sugar

1 tablespoon vegetable oil

2 teaspoons Dijon mustard

¼ teaspoon celery seeds

3 cups finely shredded green cabbage

2 carrots, shredded

salt and pepper

1. To make the pulled pork, preheat the oven to 300°F.

2. Place the onion slices in the bottom of a large cast-iron dutch oven or casserole dish. In a small bowl, combine the sugar, paprika, 1 teaspoon salt, and ½ teaspoon pepper. Rub the mixture all over the pork, then place the pork on top of the onion. Put the vinegar, Worcestershire sauce, crushed red pepper, sugar, dry mustard, and garlic into a bowl and mix together. Pour half the mixture over the pork, reserving the remainder for serving. Cover the casserole and cook in the preheated oven for about 6 hours, or until the meat is tender and falling from the bone.

3. Meanwhile, make the coleslaw. Put the vinegar, sugar, oil, Dijon mustard, 1 teaspoon salt, ½ teaspoon pepper, and celery seeds in a large bowl and beat together until emulsified. Add the cabbage and carrot and toss to combine. Cover and refrigerate until ready to serve.

4. When the meat is falling from the bone and shreds easily with a fork, remove it from the oven and discard any bones and large pieces of fat. Shred the meat using two forks. Moisten the meat to taste with the reserved vinegar mixture (any remaining sauce may be passed around at the table). Keep the meat warm on the stove until ready to serve.

5. Top the hot fries with the pulled pork and coleslaw and serve immediately.

Tangy, spicy, and sweet slow-cooked pork and crunchy coleslaw are a delightful combination on their own. On top of our classic Hand-Cut Fries, they are truly to die for.

Fries with Gravy

SERVES **4** PREP **20** COOK **35** MINUTES

INGREDIENTS

2 tablespoons
unsalted butter

2 tablespoons
all-purpose flour

2 cups beef stock, chicken
stock, or vegetable stock

½ teaspoon salt

freshly cooked Hand-Cut
Fries (see page 10)

2 cups diced Muenster
cheese, mozzarella cheese,
or cheddar cheese

pepper, to taste

1. Melt the butter in a saucepan over medium heat. Sprinkle in the flour and cook, beating continuously, for 6–8 minutes, until the mixture turns a light brown and begins to smell a bit nutty. Slowly beat in the stock, add the salt, increase the heat to high, and bring to a boil. Reduce the heat to medium–low and simmer, stirring occasionally, for 20–25 minutes, until thickened.

2. Arrange the fries on a serving platter, pour the gravy over them, and top with the cheese. Season with pepper and serve immediately.

We've given the classic French-Canadian dish known as *Poutine* a modern twist by replacing the cheese curds with muenster cheese—you could also try mozzarella cheese or cheddar cheese.

Parmesan Fries

SERVES **4** PREP **20** COOK **10** MINUTES

INGREDIENTS

freshly cooked Hand-Cut Fries (see page 10)

1 cup freshly grated Parmesan cheese, to serve

GREMOLATA

¼ cup finely chopped flat-leaf parsley

3 garlic cloves, finely chopped

finely grated zest of 1 lemon

½ teaspoon salt

1. To make the gremolata, put the parsley, garlic, lemon zest, and salt into a mortar and pound together with a pestle until fluffy (alternatively, you can crush them together on a cutting board using the side of a large knife or the back of a spoon).

2. Place the hot fries in a large bowl or on a serving platter. Sprinkle the cheese over the fries, and then sprinkle the gremolata over the top. Serve immediately.

Garlic fries go Italian
in this simple yet
sophisticated take.

42

Truffle Waffle Fries

SERVES **PREP** **COOK**
4 15 15 MINUTES

INGREDIENTS

8 russet potatoes
(about 2 pounds),
unpeeled

6 cups vegetable oil

1 tablespoon truffle oil

1 teaspoon truffle salt
or sea salt

2 tablespoons
finely chopped fresh
flat-leaf parsley

¾ cup freshly grated
Parmesan cheese

1. Cut the potatoes using the waffle blade of a handheld mandoline. Soak the cut potatoes in a bowl of cold water for 5 minutes, drain, rinse, and wrap in a clean dish towel to dry.

2. Place the vegetable oil in a large, heavy saucepan or a deep-fryer. If using a saucepan, attach a deep-frying thermometer. Heat the oil to 350–375°F, or until a cube of bread browns in 30 seconds. Carefully add the cut potatoes, in batches, if necessary, to avoid overcrowding. Cook for 3–4 minutes, until beginning to brown. Remove, using tongs, and drain on a plate lined with paper towels. Cook the next batch in the same manner.

3. Reheat the oil to 350–375°F, then add the potatoes and fry for a second time, for 3–5 minutes, until golden brown and crisp. Remove from the oil and drain on a plate lined with paper towels. Toss the hot fries with the truffle oil. Sprinkle with the salt, parsley, and the grated Parmesan cheese. Serve immediately.

Truffle salt is available online and makes these decadent waffle fries even more of a treat! Alternatively, use sea salt and the result will still be deliciously indulgent.

Wild Mushroom Fries

SERVES **PREP** **COOK**
4 **25** **30** MINUTES

INGREDIENTS

2 tablespoons olive oil

2 shallots, diced

1½ pounds assorted wild mushrooms, such as porcini, chanterelles, morels, or oyster mushrooms

1 teaspoon salt

1 cup heavy cream

¼ cup freshly grated Parmesan cheese

3 slices good-quality white bread

1 tablespoon butter

freshly cooked Hand-Cut Fries (see page 10) or Duck-Fat Fries (see page 50)

1 tablespoon finely chopped fresh thyme, to garnish

1. Heat the oil in a skillet over medium–high heat. Add the shallots and cook, stirring occasionally, for about 5 minutes until soft. Add the mushrooms and salt and continue to cook, stirring frequently, for an additional 5 minutes, until soft. Stir in the cream and bring the mixture to a boil. Reduce the heat to low and simmer, stirring occasionally, for about 5 minutes, until the sauce thickens. Remove from the heat and stir in the cheese.

2. Put the bread into a food processor and pulse to make crumbs. Melt the butter in a saucepan over medium heat. Add the bread crumbs and cook, stirring frequently, for about 3 minutes, until just beginning to brown. Remove from the heat.

3. Arrange the fries on a serving platter and spoon the sauce over them. Sprinkle the bread crumbs over the top, garnish with the thyme, and serve immediately.

If wild mushrooms are hard to find, substitute cultivated mushrooms along with dried porcini that have been soaked in hot water for 30 minutes. Add the soaking liquid to the mixture with the cream.

Duck-Fat Fries

SERVES **4** PREP **15** COOK **10** MINUTES

INGREDIENTS

8 russet potatoes
(about 2 pounds)

4 cups rendered duck fat

sea salt, to taste

1. Peel the potatoes, if desired, and cut into ¼ x ¼-inch sticks. Soak the cut potatoes in a bowl of cold water for 5 minutes, then drain, rinse, and wrap in a clean dish towel to dry.

2. Place the fat in a large, heavy saucepan or a deep-fryer. If using a saucepan, attach a deep-frying thermometer. Heat the fat to 350–375°F, or until a cube of bread browns in 30 seconds. Carefully add the cut potatoes, in batches, if necessary, to avoid overcrowding. Cook for about 3–4 minutes, until beginning to brown. Remove, using tongs, and drain on a plate lined with paper towels.

3. Reheat the fat to 350–375°F, then add the potatoes and fry for a second time, this time for about 3–5 minutes, until golden brown and crisp. Remove from the oil and drain on a plate lined with paper towels. Season generously with salt and serve immediately.

It's hard to improve on perfection, but we have to admit our classic Hand-Cut Fries are even better when they're fried in duck fat.

Cheesy Polenta Fries

INGREDIENTS

POLENTA FRIES

2 cups milk

3 cups water

2 tablespoons butter,
plus extra for greasing

1 teaspoon salt

2 cups polenta

1 cup shredded fontina
cheese, provolone cheese,
or Swiss cheese

6 cups vegetable oil

SPICY TOMATO SAUCE

2 tablespoons olive oil

1 shallot, diced

2 garlic cloves,
finely chopped

1 teaspoon crushed
red pepper

1 (14½-ounce) can
diced tomatoes

½ teaspoon salt

1 bay leaf

2 tablespoons finely
chopped fresh oregano

1. Lightly grease a 13 x 9-inch baking dish with butter. Put the milk, water, butter, and salt into a large saucepan and stir to combine. Set over medium–high heat and bring to a boil. Beat in the polenta and bring to simmering point. Reduce the heat to low and cook, stirring frequently, for about 8–10 minutes, until the polenta is thick and thoroughly cooked. Remove from the heat, stir in the cheese, and spread in the prepared baking dish. Cover and refrigerate for at least 60 minutes or up to 24 hours.

2. To make the sauce, heat the oil in a skillet over medium–high heat. Add the shallot and garlic and cook, stirring frequently, for about 5 minutes, until soft. Add the crushed red pepper and cook for an additional 30 seconds. Stir in the tomatoes, salt, and bay leaf, and bring to a boil. Reduce the heat to low and simmer, stirring occasionally, for 30 minutes. Remove the bay leaf and stir in the oregano. (The sauce may be made up to two days ahead and stored, tightly covered, in the refrigerator. Reheat on the stove before serving.)

3. Slice the chilled polenta into french-fry-shaped sticks, about ¼ inch thick. Place the oil in a large, heavy saucepan or a deep-fryer. If using a saucepan, attach a deep-frying thermometer. Heat the oil to 350–375°F, or until a cube of bread browns in 30 seconds. Carefully add the polenta sticks, in batches, if necessary, to avoid overcrowding. Cook for about 4–5 minutes, until golden brown and crisp. Remove, using tongs, and drain on a plate lined with paper towels. Serve hot with a bowl of the warm spicy tomato sauce for dipping.

These crispy, creamy, fries are a nice alternative to the standard fried potato.

Thai Red Fries

SERVES **4** PREP **15** COOK **30** MINUTES

INGREDIENTS

2 tablespoons vegetable oil, plus extra for greasing

2 tablespoons packed light brown sugar

2 tablespoons Thai fish sauce

2 tablespoons lime juice

1 tablespoon Thai red curry paste

½ teaspoon cayenne pepper (optional)

8 russet potatoes (about 2 pounds)

CILANTRO KETCHUP

1 garlic clove

¼ cup fresh cilantro

1 cup ketchup

2 tablespoons lime juice

1. Preheat the oven to 450°F. Grease a large baking sheet with oil.

2. Put the oil, sugar, fish sauce, lime juice, curry paste, and cayenne pepper, if using, into a mixing bowl and stir together until well combined.

3. Peel the potatoes, if desired, and cut them into ¼ x ¼-inch sticks. Add them to the mixture in the bowl and toss to coat. Let stand for about 5 minutes, then, using a slotted spoon, transfer the potatoes to the prepared baking sheet, letting the excess marinade run off into the bowl. Spread the potatoes in a single layer. Bake in the preheated oven for 25–30 minutes, turning after about 15 minutes, until brown and crisp.

4. Meanwhile, to make the ketchup, chop the garlic and cilantro in a food processor. Add the ketchup and lime juice and process until well combined. Transfer to a serving bowl.

5. Serve the fries hot with the ketchup for dipping.

These unusual oven-baked fries hit all the right taste buds—sweet, spicy, tangy, salty, and all-around delicious.

Spanish Fries

SERVES   PREP   COOK

4 20 20 MINUTES

INGREDIENTS

1 tablespoon olive oil

1 small onion, diced

1 garlic clove, finely chopped

8 ounces Spanish chorizo, finely diced

freshly cooked Hand-Cut Fries (see page 10)

1 cup shredded Manchego cheese, Monterey Jack cheese, or mozzarella cheese

2 tablespoons finely chopped fresh flat-leaf parsley and ½ teaspoon smoked paprika, to garnish

1. Heat the oil in a skillet over medium–high heat. Add the onion and cook, stirring frequently, for about 5 minutes, until soft. Add the garlic and chorizo and cook, stirring occasionally, for about 5 minutes, until the meat is browned.

2. Arrange the fries on a serving platter and top with the onions, chorizo, garlic, and cheese. Garnish with the parsley and paprika and serve immediately.

These sophisticated fries are more tapas bar than snack bar.

Lobster Fries

SERVES **PREP** **COOK**
4 **30** **10** MINUTES

INGREDIENTS

1 celery stalk, finely chopped

3 scallions, finely sliced

¼ cup finely chopped fresh parsley

2 tablespoons ketchup

2 tablespoons Dijon mustard

1 tablespoon prepared horseradish

1 tablespoon lemon juice

1 tablespoon paprika

1 teaspoon Worcestershire sauce

1 teaspoon hot pepper sauce

¾ cup mayonnaise

freshly cooked Hand-Cut Fries (see page 10)

1 pound cooked lobster meat, chopped into bite-size pieces

2 tablespoons snipped chives, to garnish

1. Put the celery, scallions, parsley, ketchup, mustard, horseradish, lemon juice, paprika, Worcestershire sauce, and hot pepper sauce into a bowl and mix together well. Beat in the mayonnaise until well combined. Cover and chill until ready to serve.

2. Place the hot fries on a serving platter or divide into individual serving bowls. Top with the sauce and sprinkle the lobster meat over the top. Garnish with the chives and serve immediately.

Our classic Hand-Cut Fries get presidential treatment with the addition of succulent lobster meat and a zesty sauce.

Blini Fries

SERVES **6** PREP **10** COOK **12** MINUTES

INGREDIENTS

6 russet potatoes,
(about 1½ pounds),
scrubbed or peeled and
cut into thin circles

6 cups vegetable oil

½ cup sour cream
or crème fraîche

2 ounces red or
black caviar

2 tablespoons snipped
chives, to garnish

salt, to taste

1. Soak the sliced potatoes in a large bowl of cold water for about 5 minutes. Drain and rinse the potatoes, then spread them out in a single layer on a clean dish towel. Top with another clean dish towel and press to absorb any excess water.

2. Place the oil in a large, heavy saucepan or a deep-fryer. If using a saucepan, attach a deep-frying thermometer. Heat the oil to 350–375°F, or until a cube of bread browns in 30 seconds. Carefully add the sliced potatoes, in batches, if necessary, to avoid overcrowding. Cook for about 5–6 minutes, until golden brown and crisp. Remove, using tongs, and drain on a plate lined with paper towels. Season generously with salt.

3. Arrange the fried potato slices on a serving platter and top with a spoonful of sour cream, a small spoonful of caviar, and a sprinkling of chives.

For an equally delicious alternative, substitute
strips of smoked salmon, draped
attractively over the sour cream,
for some or all of the caviar.

Homemade Ketchup

SERVES **4**   PREP **10**   COOK **20** MINUTES

INGREDIENTS

MAKES ABOUT 1 CUP

2 tablespoons olive oil

1 red onion, peeled and chopped

2 garlic cloves, chopped

4 plum tomatoes, chopped

1 cup canned diced tomatoes

½ teaspoon ground ginger

½ teaspoon chili powder

3 tablespoons packed dark brown sugar

½ cup red wine vinegar

salt and pepper, to taste

1. Heat the olive oil in a large saucepan and add the onion, garlic, and all of the tomatoes. Add the ginger and chili powder and season with salt and pepper. Cook for 15 minutes or until soft. Pour the mixture into a food processor or blender and process until well blended. Strain thoroughly to remove all the seeds. Return the mixture to the pan and add the sugar and vinegar. Return to a boil and cook until it is the consistency of ketchup.

2. Pour quickly into a clean sterilized jar and store in the refrigerator for up to one week.

Ketchup is a particularly popular condiment,
but people don't think about making their own.
This recipe is surprisingly quick,
easy and tastes absolutely superb.

Aioli

SERVES **4** PREP **10** COOK **0** MINUTES

PLUS CHILLING

INGREDIENTS

MAKES ABOUT 1 CUP

3 large garlic cloves, finely chopped

2 egg yolks

1 cup extra-virgin olive oil

1 tablespoon lemon juice

1 tablespoon lime juice

1 tablespoon Dijon mustard

1 tablespoon chopped fresh tarragon

salt and pepper, to taste

fresh tarragon sprig, to garnish

1. Make sure that all the ingredients are at room temperature. Place the garlic and egg yolks in a food processor and process until well blended. With the motor running, pour in the oil, one teaspoon at a time, through the feeder tube until the mixture starts to thicken, then pour in the remaining oil in a thin stream until a thick mayonnaise forms.

2. Add the lemon juice, lime juice, mustard, and tarragon and season with salt and pepper. Blend until smooth, then transfer to a nonmetallic bowl. Garnish with a tarragon sprig. Cover with plastic wrap and refrigerate for up to one to two days..

This popular French-style garlic mayonnaise goes
perfectly with our freshly cooked Hand-Cut
Fries (see page 10).

Barbecue Sauce

SERVES **4**   PREP **15**   COOK **20** MINUTES

INGREDIENTS

MAKES ABOUT 1 CUP

1 tablespoon olive oil

1 small onion, finely chopped

2–3 garlic cloves, crushed

1 fresh red jalapeño chile, seeded and finely chopped (optional)

2 teaspoons tomato paste

1 teaspoon dry mustard, or to taste

1 tablespoon red-wine vinegar

1 tablespoon Worcestershire sauce

2–3 teaspoons packed brown sugar

1¼ cups water

1. Heat the oil in a small, heavy saucepan, add the onion, garlic, and chile, if using, and gently sauté, stirring frequently, for 3 minutes, or until beginning to soften. Remove from the heat.

2. Blend the tomato paste with the dry mustard, red-wine vinegar, and Worcestershire sauce to a paste, then stir into the onion mixture with 2 teaspoons of the sugar. Mix well, then gradually stir in the water.

3. Return to the heat and bring to a boil, stirring frequently. Reduce the heat and gently simmer, stirring occasionally, for 15 minutes. Taste and add the remaining sugar, if desired. Strain, if preferred, and serve hot or let cool and serve cold.

Although barbecue sauce is usually associated with meat, it goes perfectly with fries—try with our Cajun Fries (see page 32).

Blue Cheese Dip

SERVES **4**   PREP **10**   COOK **0** MINUTES

INGREDIENTS

1 cup cream cheese

1 cup sour cream

⅓ cup finely crumbled, firm blue cheese

1 scallion, white part only, finely chopped

1 tablespoon chopped fresh parsley

1 tablespoon chopped fresh thyme

salt and pepper, to taste

1. Put the cream cheese and sour cream into a large bowl and beat well.

2. Add the blue cheese, scallion, parsley, and thyme and stir until combined. Season with salt and pepper.

3. Transfer to individual serving bowls and serve.

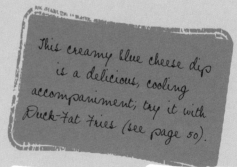

This creamy blue cheese dip is a delicious, cooling accompaniment; try it with Duck-Fat Fries (see page 50).

Curry Mustard Dip

SERVES **4** PREP **5** COOK **0** MINUTES

INGREDIENTS

MAKES ABOUT 1 CUP
½ cup sour cream

¼ cup Dijon mustard

¼ cup lemon juice

2 tablespoons
curry powder

1. Put the sour cream and mustard into a medium bowl and stir until well combined. Add the lemon juice and curry powder and stir to mix well.

2. To store, cover and refrigerate for up to a week.

This simple dip is best made a few hours ahead. Keep it refrigerated and bring to room temperature before serving.

Ranch Dressing

SERVES **4**   PREP **5**   COOK **0** MINUTES

INGREDIENTS

MAKES ABOUT 2 CUPS

¾ cup buttermilk

¾ cup sour cream

2 tablespoons finely chopped fresh flat-leaf parsley

2 tablespoons finely chopped scallions

2 tablespoons finely chopped celery

2 teaspoons finely chopped fresh dill

1 tablespoon lemon juice

1 garlic clove, finely chopped

½ teaspoon dry mustard

½ teaspoon salt

½ teaspoon pepper

1. Put the buttermilk and sour cream into a bowl and mix until well combined. Add the remaining ingredients and stir to mix well.

2. To store, cover and refrigerate for up to a week.

Packed with a host of fresh herbs, creamy ranch dressing is a surprisingly refreshing dip for your favorite style of fries.

Basil Pesto

SERVES **4**   PREP **10**   COOK **0** MINUTES

INGREDIENTS

MAKES ABOUT 1 CUP

1¼ cups fresh basil leaves

1 garlic clove

3 tablespoons toasted pine nuts

½–⅔ cup extra-virgin olive oil

¼ cup freshly grated Parmesan cheese

1–2 teaspoons freshly squeezed lemon juice (optional)

salt and pepper, to taste

1. Tear the basil leaves and put in a large mortar with the garlic, pine nuts, and 1 tablespoon of the oil. Pound with a pestle to form a paste.

2. Gradually work in the remaining oil to form a thick sauce. Add salt and pepper and stir in the Parmesan cheese. If desired, thin slightly with the lemon juice.

Try varying the amounts of the garlic,
cheese, basil, or lemon juice in this
dip to suit your own taste.

Spicy Salsa

SERVES **4** PREP **10** COOK **20** MINUTES

INGREDIENTS

MAKES ABOUT 2 CUPS

vegetable oil spray

8 plum tomatoes, halved

2–4 jalapeños, to taste,
halved, cored, and seeded

4 garlic cloves

1 large onion,
cut into wedges

¼ cup fresh cilantro

¼ cup lime juice

salt, to taste

1. Preheat the oven to 450°F and spray a baking sheet with oil.

2. Place the tomatoes, jalapeños, garlic, and onion on the prepared baking sheet and lightly spray with oil. Sprinkle with a little salt and roast in the preheated oven for about 15–20 minutes, until the vegetables soften and begin to brown.

3. Place the vegetables in a food processor and pulse to a chunky puree. Add the cilantro, lime juice, and 1 teaspoon of salt and pulse until the cilantro is chopped and all of the ingredients are well combined.

4. To store, cover and refrigerate for up to a week.

This spicy roasted salsa is a great dip for our Seasoned Curly Fries (see page 18), or use it to top our Nacho Fries (see page 30).